DIY Protein Bars At Home

*31 Simple, Delicious And Nutritious
Homemade Energy Bar, Granola Bar
And Protein Bar Recipes*

Jessica David

COPYRIGHT

DISCLAIMER

Your Free Gift

As a special Thank You for downloading this book I have put together an exclusive report on "Superfoods For Weight Loss" which includes a checklist, recipes and a diet map.

Learn about simple Superfoods that will not only help you lose weight but also, strengthen your body and improve mental performance. These foods are packed with nutrients, antioxidants and have amazing side bonuses – like cancer fighting agents. This free report includes a Superfood checklist and an easy to follow diet schedule.

>> You Can Download This Free Report By Clicking Here <<

Kindle 5 Star Books

Free Kindle 5 Star Book Club Membership

Join Other Kindle 5 Star Members Who Are Getting Private Access To
Weekly Free Kindle Book Promotions

Get free Kindle books

Stay connected:

Join our Facebook group

Follow Kindle 5 Star on Twitter

Also, if you want to receive updates on Jessica David's new books, free
promotions and Kindle countdown deals sign up to her New Release
Mailing List.

Table of Contents

Introduction

Chapter 1 - What Are Protein Bars?

Chapter 2 - Great Recipes

Berry-Berry Blue Breakfast Bars

Easy No Bake Protein Bar

Greek Yoghurt and Vanilla Blueberry Granola Bars

Chewy, Gooey, Soft Granola Protein Bars

No Bake Fudgie Vegan Oatmeal Bars

No Bake Fudgy, Chocolatey Energy Bites

Pretzel and Peanut Butter Bars

Ripe Strawberry Protein Bars

Vanilla & Ginger Crunchy Protein Bars

Raisin and Oatmeal Protein Bars

Vegan Choco Almond Bars

Coconut Cherry and Almond Protein Bites

Dark Chocolate with Coconut Protein Balls

Whole Grain with Raspberry Jam Bars

Peanut Butter with Chia Seeds Protein Balls

Nutritious Banana Bars

Almond and Coconut Bars

No Bake Crumbled Quinoa Bars

Coconut and Strawberry Granola Bars

Nutritious Homemade Granola Bars

Sweet, Chewy & Crunchy Homemade Bars

Nuts and Dried Fruit Granola Bars

Sweet Peppermint Bars with Dates

Blueberry and Banana Protein Bars

Chewy & Nutty Energy Bars

Triple Choco-Oatmeal Cookie Bars

Peanut Butter and Oatmeal Honey Bars

Dark Chocolate with Pretzel Bars

Protein Rich Banana Bread Bars

No Bake Vegan & Gluten Free Protein Bars

No Bake Granolas with M&M, Pretzels and Peanut Butter

No Bake White Choco Protein Bars

Buckwheat and Blueberry Granola Bars

Hemp Protein Rich Granola Bars

Protein Pumpkin Bread Bars

Conclusion

Introduction

In today's society, people are always on the go – everything is fast paced. Change is inevitable. Due to this very busy state, a lot of people tend to skip meals and forget to eat. That's the reason why a lot of people are starting to have unhealthy diets, ulcers, stomach problems and other diseases, which the body acquires because of this simple neglect.

Not to worry though because you are holding in your hand a book that would help you make healthy yet fulfilling snacks to suit your busy schedule and fast paced lifestyle. Health buffs especially will want to have a snack at hand if they are on the gym.

Thank you for your purchase of this book: *DIY Protein Bars At Home: Simple, Delicious And Nutritious Homemade Energy Bar, Granola Bar And Protein Bar Recipes.* In this book I will provide you an overview of protein bars and its benefit. But most of all you will discover how simple and easy it is to learn how to make them yourself.

Having a nutritious snack at hand is very important to keeping your metabolism energized the whole day. With protein bars you are able to eat while you are on the road, in a meeting and even while you are exercising.

Put on your apron and cooking hat because you are about to discover, learn and prepare delicious protein bar recipes!

Let's get busy and enjoy!

Chapter 1 - What Are Protein Bars?

Nowadays, protein bars are becoming one of the most popular ways to enjoy a healthy snack that often includes oats, nuts, fruits and other superfoods. The health benefit of protein bars is an important selling point for health conscious shoppers who want to lose weight. Since they are so simple to make and so delicious to eat, granola bars, energy bars and protein bars have become the new stars when it comes to healthy snacking.

Eating protein bars is an easy and new way of getting some extra amount of protein into your body and diet. They can either help you lose weight or gain weight. A serving of a protein in between your meals can help you control your appetite. Just remember like any other food, do not eat too much because there are protein bars that have a lot of sugars and calories. Look for the ones that are lower in both sugar and calorie content. So make sure that you will be reading them first before buying it.

Most of the protein bars in the market use whey or soy proteins. Whey proteins are considered to be the "complete protein" because it has low lactose content and contains 9 important amino acids. Aside from this essential nutrients being given by protein, it has many benefits like lowering cholesterol, asthma, for losing weight and lower the risks of having heart diseases.

Proteins are important for the body because it helps build muscles. More muscles means less fat will be accumulated in the body. It also aids in the improvement of brain functions and can help you lose weight.

What are the benefits of protein bars?

As mentioned because of the fast paced movement in society many people are too busy to have a decent meal. The main benefit of baking protein bars market is for convenience. People on the go will have a nutritious replacement for the meals they miss. It provides healthy replacement for snacks instead of eating processed foods.

Protein bars are also best for people who are into bodybuilding or are following a high protein diet. The ingredients within the bars help to build leaner muscles and also give an additional protein boost. People who also want to lose weight find protein bars a good replacement for sweet cravings or snacks. Since they are already filled with good nutrients, they are a complete meal in itself. What's more, they can also be filling and can satisfy your hunger until your next real meal.

The only downsize of buying protein bars in the market is simply not knowing the real ingredients included in the product. There have been studies that show "many" protein bars that are not truly fat free. You will be surprised that there are a number of products that have high calories because they are high in added sugar. Since soy proteins and processed whey do not taste good, manufacturers add low calorie sweeteners in order to make the taste bearable for the consumers. In the end, some side effects would include upset stomach but the bad thing about it is that it's not calorie or fat free at all. So make sure that you read all the labels carefully before buying that particular protein bar.

However the best way to make sure that all ingredients are according to your taste and no additives are included is to – MAKE your OWN protein bars!

Making your own protein or granola bars is a fun and exciting way to monitor the calories that are absorbed by the body. Not to mention, you will be able to choose the ingredients that you want, also adjust the amount of sugar. Maybe you will convince your family and friends to follow your healthy lifestyle. Not bad, huh?

So move along now and check out the wonderful recipes I've prepared on the succeeding chapter. Enjoy and have fun creating them! Just a request though - Make sure to share these delicious and healthy bars to your friends and loved ones. Let's start baking and creating!

Chapter 2 - Great Recipes

Welcome and step into my kitchen. You will now have the chance to create delicious and nutritious protein; make energy and granola bars in your own home. Not to mention this will be an additional workout for you and an exciting activity that you can share with others.

Here are the great recipes you have been waiting for!

Berry-Berry Blue Breakfast Bars

Ingredients

- 1 ½ cups 100% pure rolled oats
- ½ cup of blueberries (dried)
- ¾ cups of almonds (whole)
- ½ cup of pistachios
- 1 /3 cups flaxseed (ground)
- 1/3 of walnuts
- 1/3 cup of pepitas
- ¼ cup of sunflower seeds
- 1/3 cup of pure honey (you can also use maple syrup)
- ¼ cup of apple sauce (unsweetened)
- 1 cup of almond butter

Directions

1)   Place parchment paper or wax paper in your baking pan that is

about 8x8 in size, leaving the paper hang over the edges.

2)   Combine rolled oats, almonds, blueberries, pistachios, flaxseed, walnuts, pepitas and sunflower seeds in a large sized bowl and mix them all together.

3)   Slowly add the honey and continue to lightly stir. Then add the almond butter and mix them well.

4)   Place the batter mix in the lined baking pan and press it firmly using the palm of your hands or if you have a mini roller, you can use that as well. Make sure that it's evenly distributed and rolled.

5)   Freeze for about an hour. Remove from the freezer and slowly lift the paper with the portion of the mixture. Gently peel the paper and slice it diagonally to long bars, this would make at least 8 bars. Cut them into half to create 16 bars. Place them on a reseal-able bag and put them on the freezer.

6)   When you are in a hurry, just get a piece and voila! Enjoy! Makes 16 delicious bars.

Easy No Bake Protein Bar

Ingredients

- 5 tablespoons of your choice of peanut butter (choose the natural variety of either smooth or chunky)

- ½ cup of dry oats (you can also use uncooked whole grain cereals)

- ½ cup of oat flour (if you don't have oat flour, double the amount of the oats)

- 6 scoops of low carbohydrate whey protein (chocolate flavor; you can also use 132 grams of protein as replacement)

- 1 tsp. vanilla extract

- 2 tbs. of flaxseed (optional)

- 1 cup of dry milk (non-fat)

- ½ cup of water (amount depends on what type of protein you will use)

Directions

1)   Prepare an 8x8 size baking pan and spray some cooking spray.

2)   In a medium bowl, mix all together all the dry ingredients. Then add your peanut butter and start mixing. This will become dry and crumbly. Add the water and vanilla. Mix well using a rubber spatula or a wooden spoon. Make sure to mix thoroughly until it forms into a dough. Dough will become sticky. Spread the dough you created in the baking pan using your clean spatula or wooden spoon. Refrigerate your mixture for a number of hours or you can choose to freeze the mixture for about an hour. Once hardened, cut them into 9 squares.

3)   Wrap the squares individually or you can store them and cover them in a container putting sheets in between the wax paper. Keep them refrigerated.

4)   Just get a piece when you want to eat them. Enjoy! Makes 9-10 squares.

Greek Yoghurt and Vanilla Blueberry Granola Bars

Ingredients

- 2 cups rolled oats (preferably gluten free)

- 1 ½ cup of rice krispies (brown rice preferred)

- ¼ cup of unsweetened coconut (shredded)

- ¼ cup of whole almonds (roasted and chopped roughly)

- 1 tbs. chia seeds

- ¼ tsp. salt

- ½ cup of peanut or almond butter

- ½ cup of honey

- 1 ½ teaspoon of vanilla

- 1 cup of fresh blueberries (you can also use ¾ cups of dried blueberries)

For the Greek Yogurt Glaze Coating

- 1 tbs. water

- 1 tsp. vanilla

- ½ teaspoon of gelatin

- ½ cup of Greek yogurt

- 1 tablespoon of honey

- A dash of salt

- 2 cups of refined powdered sugar

Directions

1)   Pre-heat the oven to about 350 degrees. (*If you will use dried blueberries, you can skip this procedure)

2)   Place wax or parchment paper in a baking tray and spread your blueberries on it. Roast for about 30 to 40 min. or until your berries shrink and burst. Remove the tray from the oven and let it cool.

3)   Prepare and place wax or parchment paper in a 9x13 baking pan.

4)   In a large sized bowl, mix the rice krispies, oats, coconuts, chia seeds, almonds and salt. Mix well.

5)   In a separate mixing bowl, mix honey and almond butter. Heat inside the microwave for about 30 seconds to a minute or until the mixture becomes liquid and can be poured. Add vanilla and mix it again.

6)   Add the honey mixture into the oats mixture and combine well. Make sure that everything is well combined and moist. Gently add the blueberries. Press mixture in the prepared baking pan. Press firmly using the back of a cup or spatula.

7)   Freeze the mixture for about an hour. Once hardened, cut them into 9 to 12 bars and return it inside the freezer.

8)   To make the yogurt coating: mix vanilla and water in a small sized bowl. Sprinkle gelatin on top and using a fork, whisk it until gelatin becomes evenly distributed. Set aside until it is time to use. This will set and become a thick paste.

9)   In another small sized bowl, whisk honey, yogurt and salt. Microwave for about 15 seconds, stir it occasionally until yogurt becomes warm and liquid in form. Make sure that you will not boil yogurt or else this will curdled.

10)   In this warm yogurt mixture, add the gelatin and whisk until gelatin is dissolved completely. Scrape and transfer yogurt mixture to a medium sized mixing bowl. Add powdered sugar and mix until thoroughly combined. Appearance should look like a thick coating but

can still be poured.

11)   Line another wax paper on a baking tray. Dip the bar one at a time on the yogurt mixture. Flip and face the dipped side upward and place on the baking tray. Allow excess mixture to drip off. This would be very sticky. Repeat same procedure on remaining bars. Once done, let it sit for a few minutes until it would become dry when you touch it, preferably overnight to make sure that it is dried thoroughly. Cover remaining yogurt mixture until you will be using it again.

12)   Once all the bars are dried completely, flip it over making the yogurt side faced down. Using the remaining yogurt mixture, place it on a re-sealable plastic and cut a small hole on the edge of the plastic. This should look like a pastry bag where you can squeeze the mixture and drizzle it all over the bar. Set it aside again and let sit for a few more minutes, preferable overnight once again.

13)   When coating is already dried up you can now put them on individual wraps or place on a container. This makes 8-12 bars.

14)   Whenever you are ready to go, get a piece and enjoy!

Chewy, Gooey, Soft Granola Protein Bars

Ingredients

- 2 cups of quick oats

- ½ cup of protein powder (preferably vanilla flavor; you can also use whey)

- 2 tablespoons of ground flax

- 1 tsp. cinnamon

- ¼ tsp. salt

- ¼ cup of almond butter (or any kind of nut butter)

- ¼ cup of honey

- ½ cup of almond milk (vanilla flavor or you can also use any kind of milk)

- 1 teaspoon of vanilla

- 1/3 cup mini sized chocolate chips

Directions:

1)   Pre-heat the oven to about 350 degrees.

2)   Prepare an 8x8 size baking pan and spray some cooking spray.

3)   In a large sized mixing bowl, combine protein powder, oats, cinnamon, flax and salt. Set them aside.

4)   Meanwhile in another medium mixing bowl, mix honey, almond butter and milk and also the vanilla. Combine them well. Pour the wet mixture over the dry one that you've set aside. Mix gently until all ingredients are fully combined. Gently fold in the chocolate chips.

5)   Pour this mixture on the pan that you prepared and spread mixture evenly using your hands or a spatula. Press it down firmly.

6)   Bake for about 18-20 minutes or until the edges become golden brown.

7)   Once done, remove from the oven and let cool for about 20 minutes.

8)   Cut the cooked mixture into bars. This would make around 12 bars.

9)   Keep in container or wrap individually until ready to eat and take wherever you want. Enjoy!

No Bake Fudgie Vegan Oatmeal Bars

Ingredients

To prepare crust

- 1 ½ cup of rolled oats
- ½ cup of almond flour
- ½ cup of almonds (raw)
- ¼ teaspoon of salt
- 3 tbs. rice syrup (preferably use brown rice)
- 2 tablespoons of coconut oil (melted)

To prepare the filling

- 1 cup of dates (pitted and chopped roughly)
- ¼ cup of cocoa powder (unsweetened)
- 2-4 tbs. water

Directions

1)   In an 8x8 sized baking pan, line it with an aluminum foil and leave a few inches of it to hang on the side of your pan. This would make it easier to remove the mixture on the pan. Set it aside.

2)   Using your food processor, place almond flour, oats, salt and almonds. Pulse a few minutes until consistency becomes roughly crumbled. Add the rice syrup with the coconut oil and repeat processing. Make sure that it is thoroughly mixed well until it slowly forms into dough and begins to become sticky.

3)   Reserve ½ a cup of this mixture. Transfer remaining dough to the prepared pan you've made earlier. Press it down firmly and evenly using your spatula or your fingers.

4)   Make the filling by adding cocoa powder, dates and water into your food processor. Pulse it again until the dates are thoroughly broken down to become a paste. Scrape the sides and add water if the mixture becomes too difficult to handle. Just make sure that you don't add a lot of water because you still want the mixture to be thick and pasty.

5)   Once you are satisfied with its consistency, transfer the paste on the baking pan. Spray some cooking spray to your spatula and use it to spread the paste mixture evenly on top of the oats mixture. Using the reserved oats mixture earlier, sprinkle them on top and press down using your fingers.

6)   Refrigerate it for about an hour. Cut them into bars and store in a large container or you can also wrap them individually. This would make 16 bars. Enjoy!

No Bake Fudgy, Chocolatey Energy Bites

Ingredients

• ¼ cup of oats (rolled)

• 1 cup of dates (pitted)

• 3 tablespoons of almond butter (or you can use any kind of nut butter)

• 1 tablespoon of honey

• 2 tbs. cocoa powder

• 1 scoop of protein powder (you can use any of your favorite flavor)

• ¼ cup of mini choco chips

Instructions

1)   In your food processor or a blender, put the oats and pulse until it reached the appearance of flour.

2)   Add dates, honey and almond butter. Continue to pulse and process until it is combined well. Scrape the sides and if it becomes a bit difficult to do so, add a few amount of water slowly. Make sure that you don't add too much water to avoid making the dough too sticky.

3)   Combine protein powder and cocoa and continue mixing with the processor. Mix them well.

4)   In a small sized bowl, transfer the dough and add the choco chips. Mix using your hand until it is fully combined. Using a tablespoon, divide the dough to 12 bars and roll them to form a ball. Place these balls in the refrigerator for about 20 minutes to set. This makes 12 delicious bites.

5)   Keep in container or wrap individually until ready to eat and take wherever you want. Enjoy!

Pretzel and Peanut Butter Bars

Ingredients

- 5 cups of soy crisps

- 6 tablespoons of protein powder (soy variety)

- 6 tablespoons of peanut butter (powder variety)

- ½ cup of water

- 6 tablespoons of agave

- 2 tablespoons of peanuts (chopped roughly)

- 6 pieces of pretzel twists (mini sized and chopped roughly)

- 2 tablespoons of peanut butter chips (cut into half)

Directions

1)   Prepare an 8x8 size baking pan and spray some cooking spray.

2)   Add half of soy crisps in the food processor or you can also use a blender. Pulse it around 3-4 times. Transfer to a large sized bowl and break the large pieces if there are any. Repeat the same method on the remaining crisps. Add soy powder in the bowl and mix well to distribute evenly.

3)   Add peanut butter, agave and water in a small sized pot. Cook it on low to medium heat and constantly stir using your spatula for around 3 minutes bringing it to a boil. Let boil for about 15-20 seconds and start pouring it over soy mixture. Stir using the spatula to make sure that all dry ingredients are well combined.

4)   Pour mixture in the prepared baking pan and firmly press it down. Sprinkle them (according to the correct order) with peanuts then pretzels then peanut butter chips on top. Press each of them down in the mixture. This makes 10 bars.

5)   Keep in container or wrap individually until ready to eat and take

wherever you want. Enjoy!

Ripe Strawberry Protein Bars

Ingredients

- 4 tablespoons of frozen dried strawberries

- 2/3 cup of coconut (unsweetened and shredded)

- 4 tablespoons of protein powder (unflavored whey)

- ½ teaspoon of vanilla

- 4 tablespoons of coconut milk (unsweetened and you can also use almond milk)

- 7 2/3 tablespoons of dark chocolate

Directions

1)   Using a food processor, place the strawberries and pulse until they are ground finely. Add in the whey and coconut plus vanilla and pulse again until it becomes fine but not becoming a flour texture. There should be some coarse pieces to add texture on the bar.

2)   Add coconut milk and pulse again to completely combine the mixture. Prepare a tin bar and put some silicone paper. Press down the mixture on the tin, cover and refrigerate until it becomes firm and forms into a bar.

3)   Put the pieces of dark chocolate in a microwave-safe container and microwave it for about a minute or until it is melted. Keep stirring until it slowly cools down. You can also melt the chocolate using a double broiler or use a bowl and place them on hot water. Once the chocolate is fully melted, stir and let cool.

4)   Coat each of the bars in the melted chocolate and let it set. Place them on the refrigerator for about 10 minutes or until chocolate already sets. This would make 4 big bars or 8 small ones.

5)   Keep in container or wrap individually until ready to eat and take wherever you want. Enjoy!

Vanilla & Ginger Crunchy Protein Bars

Ingredients

- 2 tablespoons of soy (you can use earth balance, butter or free variety)

- ¼ cup of agave nectar

- ¼ cup of coconut milk in carton

- 2 scoops of vanilla flavored protein

- 1 cup of oats

- 1 cup of corn flakes (you can choose your favorite brand)

- ½ cup of almonds (raw and chopped)

- ¼ cup of sunflower seeds

- ½ cup of ginger (crystallized and chopped)

- ¼ cup of coconut (shredded)

Directions

1) Over low to medium heat melt the butter in a saucepan. Whisk the agave in and add milk with the protein powder. Whisk them well until they are smooth.

2) In a large sized bowl, add the oats, almonds, sunflower seeds, cornflakes, and about ¾ of the ginger pieces. Pour in the melted butter over them and mix well.

3) Place a parchment paper or aluminum foil and spray cooking spray in a 9x9 baking tray. You can then transfer the mixture in the tray and press it down firmly with wet hands to spread evenly.

4) Sprinkle on top the shredded coconut with the remaining ginger and press it down into the bars. Bake for about 20 minutes over 325 degrees. Let it cool before cutting. This makes 9 bars.

5) Enjoy as you bring them along and snack it down.

Raisin and Oatmeal Protein Bars

Ingredients

- 3 cups of oats

- 4 scoops of vanilla flavored protein (you can also use whey)

- ¼ cup of raw almonds

- ¼ cup of raisins

- ¼ cup of butter

- 1 ¼ cup water

- ¼ cup of maple syrup

- ¼ cup of honey

- 2 eggs

Directions

1)   Preheat your oven to 350 degrees.

2)   In a large sized bowl, melt your butter and mix oats, protein powder, almonds and raisins. Set aside.

3)   Using a different bowl, combine water, honey and maple syrup. Add them on the raisin and oatmeal mixture. Mix well.

4)   Using a glass dish casserole, spray using cooking spray and add the mixture on it. Spread it evenly and bake in the oven for about 15-20 minutes until it becomes lightly brown.

5)   Remove from the oven and let it cool for about 10 minutes.

6)   Cut them into equal serving bars. This will make about 4-6 bars.

7)   Keep them on a container and if needed, get a few pieces and enjoy!

Vegan Choco Almond Bars

Ingredients

- ¼ cup of raw almonds

- ¼ tsp. sea salt

- 1 tsp. cinnamon

- 1 ½ cups of rolled oats

- 5 ounces of vanilla flavored protein

- 1/3 cup of maple syrup

- ¼ cup of chocolate chips (use dairy free variety)

Directions

1)   Prepare an 8x8 size baking pan and spray some cooking spray.

2)   Reserve about ¼ cup of almonds and chop it. Set aside.

3)   Using your food processor, add remaining almonds and salt. Pulse for several minutes until you produced almond butter.

4)   Add protein powder, maple syrup and oats. Process until it becomes smooth.

5)   Press the mixture into the baking pan using the end back part of your spoon. Top it with the chopped almonds and press them on the bars.

6)   Meanwhile, place the choco chips in a small sized glass bowl. Microwave it until it melts. Drizzle the melted chocolate over the top of the bars. Refrigerate for about 20 minutes and cool. Once cooled, cut into bars. Makes 6 bars.

7)   Store in a container and eat a few pieces in case you need another energy boost. Enjoy!

Coconut Cherry and Almond Protein Bites

Ingredients

- 1 cup of raw almonds

- 1 cup of cottage cheese

- 1 tablespoon of maple syrup

- 1 tsp. cinnamon

- 1 cup rolled oats

- ¼ cup of unsweetened coconut

- ¼ cup of dried cherries (chopped)

Directions

1)   Using your food processor, grind raw almonds until it turned into a coarsely grinded powder form. Add maple syrup, cottage cheese and cinnamon. Mix well until it forms into a paste.

2)   Mix the coconut, cherries and rolled oats in a different bowl.

3)   Add wet ingredients on the oats mixture and combine them well.

4)   Form the mixture to 18 balls and put them on a cutting board with parchment paper.

5)   Put inside the freezer for 30 min. and set.

6)   Before you eat these delicious bites, thaw them first. This makes 18 ball bites. Enjoy!

Dark Chocolate with Coconut Protein Balls

Ingredients

- ¼ cup of chia seeds

- 4 tablespoons of almond butter

- 3 tbs. of protein powder (you can use your favorite flavor)

- 3 tablespoons of dark chocolate powder

- 1/8 teaspoon of sea salt

- 1 tbs. honey (you can also use agave nectar)

- 1 tbs. of melted coconut oil

- ¼ cup of dried coconut (unsweetened and shredded)

- ½ teaspoon of vanilla extract

- ¼ cup of dried coconut (also unsweetened and shredded; for rolling)

Directions

1) Combine all of the ingredients and mix well. You can either use your hands or by food processor.

2) Once ingredients are well combined, form the dough into 1 to ½ inch of balls. Roll them on the shredded coconut and place on a baking tray. Place it on the refrigerator and let it set.

3) Once set, you can already eat and try these delicious protein balls. This makes about 9 protein balls. Enjoy!

Whole Grain with Raspberry Jam Bars

Ingredients

- Cooking spray
- 2 cups flour (whole wheat)
- ½ cup of wheat germ
- ½ cups granulated sugar
- ½ teaspoon of salt
- 2 sticks of butter (cut to 16 pieces then softened)
- ½ cup of rolled oats
- ½ cup of walnut pieces
- ¼ cup light brown sugar
- 2 tablespoons of flax seeds (ground)
- ¾ cup of raspberry jam (use the sugar free variant)
- ¾ cup of fresh raspberries
- 1 tbs. lemon juice

Directions

1) Preheat your oven to 375 degrees.

2) Prepare a 13x9 baking pan and line it with aluminum foil. Spread the 2 aluminum foil in a way that they are perpendicular to each other on the baking pan. There should be an extra aluminum foil hanging on the sides of the pan. Spray foil using the cooking spray.

3) In a large sized bowl, whisk wheat germ, flour, salt and granulated sugar. Using an electric beater, add 14 tablespoons of butter and beat together with the other ingredients for 1 ½ minutes or until it looks like a wet sand. Reserve 1 ¼ cups of this mixture to be used as a topping. Place the rest of the mixture on the baking pan and

press it down evenly using the bottom part of the measuring cup. Bake for about 14-18 minutes until edges turn brown.

4)   Combine nuts, oats, flax seeds and flour and the sugar. Add remaining butter and pinch mixture to small clumps.

5)   In a different bowl, smash raspberries lightly and combine it with lemon juice and jam. Spread this mixture on the baked crust and sprinkle on top the crumbs. Bake it again for about 22-25 minutes until it becomes golden brown.

6)   Remove from the oven. Let it cool. Once cooled, remove by lifting the hanging foil edges and place on a plate. Cut it to 24 squares.

7)   Store in a container and eat a few pieces in case you need another energy boost. Enjoy!

Peanut Butter with Chia Seeds Protein Balls

Ingredients

- 6 pieces of dates

- 1 scoop of protein powder (used natural raw)

- 4 tablespoons of peanut butter (you either use the smooth or crunchy variety)

- 2 tsp. ground chia seeds

Directions

1) Using a food processor, pulse all the ingredients until well blended.

2) Get a spoon and roll them into 10 balls. Place them on baking tray with parchment paper lining.

3) Once done forming them into balls, refrigerate and let set.

4) Store in a container and eat a few pieces in case you need another energy boost. Enjoy!

Nutritious Banana Bars

Ingredients

- ½ cup of oats
- ½ cup of protein powder
- 5 tablespoons of cream cheese(fat free variety)
- 7 tablespoons of powdered milk (skimmed)
- 2 egg whites
- 4 tablespoons of water
- 1 ½ mashed banana
- 2 teaspoons of vegetable oil
- Protein powder
- Fruits
- Oats

Directions

1) Preheat oven to 325 degrees.

2) Mix the oats, milk powder and protein powder.

3) Whisk together egg whites, cream cheese, bananas, water and oil in a different bowl. Mix well.

4) Combine all dry and wet ingredients.

5) Pour the mixture into a parchment lined baking tray on either 9x9 or 8x8 sized pan.

6) Bake for about 30-35 minutes. To check if it's fully cooked, try to pierce a toothpick in the middle. If it comes out without the mixture then it's already fully cooked.

7) Remove it from the oven and let cool. Cut into 9 square pieces.

8)   Keep them on a container and if needed, get a few pieces and enjoy!

Almond and Coconut Bars

Ingredients

- ¾ cups of almonds (toasted lightly)

- ¾ cups of cashews (toasted lightly)

- 1 ½ cups of unsweetened coconut flakes (toasted lightly)

- ½ cup of honey

- 3 tbs. water

- Pinch of sea salt

- 1 tsp. vanilla (this is optional)

- Nut varieties and seeds (sesame, chia, poppy or flax)

- Dried fruits

Directions

1)   Preheat your oven to 325 degrees.

2)   In a small sized pot, heat stove on low to medium heat and add salt, water, vanilla and honey. Heat ingredients while stirring occasionally until it starts to bubble. Reduce heat but continue to simmer until the honey reaches a heat of 270 degrees. This would take about 25 minutes on medium to low heat. Your goal is to reach the temperature of 250 degrees.

3)   While the honey mixture is simmering, toast coconut and nuts lightly inside the oven. You will know that it's done when coconut is already fragrant and a bit golden. This would take around 8-10 minutes.

4)   Once the honey mixture have reached the desired temperature, turn it off and pour the toasted coconut and nuts in the pot and stir to coat them well. Don't worry even if the mixture seemed to look dry. Keep on stirring until coated evenly. Spread it out on a lined 8x8 baking pan. Make sure to spread it evenly with your greased spatula.

Press it down firmly and compress.

5)   Cover it with parchment paper and press it down more firmly using the bottom of your cup. Make sure to compact the mixture as much as possible because this will help bars stay together while you cut the. Let it cool for about 45 minutes without any cover.

6)   Once cooled, flip and cut into bar pieces. This will make 10-12 bars.

7)   Keep them on a container and if needed, get a few pieces and enjoy!

No Bake Crumbled Quinoa Bars

Ingredients

- 1 ¼ cups of granola

- 1 cup of quinoa (cooked and let it cool)

- 1 cup of raw almonds (raw and chopped coarsely)

- ½ cup of flaxseed (ground)

- ¼ teaspoon of salt

- 1/3 cup of honey

- ¼ cup of coconut oil (melted; you can also use peanut butter)

- 1 teaspoon of vanilla extract

- ¾ cup of mini choco chips (you can also use pomegranate seeds that are dried or you can mix them)

Directions

1)   In a large sized bowl, combine granola, almonds, quinoa, salt and flaxseed. Mix them well. Add the pomegranate seeds or choco chips and fold them in.

2)   Pour the coconut butter, vanilla extract and honey and stir well. Make sure you combine the mixture thoroughly. Microwave the mixture for about 45 seconds and remove. Allow to cool and pour in the dry ingredients making the entire mixture moist. If mixture still looks dry, add an additional honey slowly. Make sure that the mixture will not be too liquid.

3)   On a 9x9 baking tray, line it with parchment or wax paper. Place the mixture and press it to the pan. Spread evenly and press it down firmly, make sure to make it as compact as possible.

4)   Refrigerate for 2 hrs. and remove from the tray. Cut it into 12 amazing squares.

5)   Keep them on a container and if needed, get a few pieces and

enjoy!

Coconut and Strawberry Granola Bars

Ingredients

- 1 pound of strawberries (small sized and cut in half)
- ½ cup of coconut oil (you may also use butter)
- ½ cup of corn syrup (light variety)
- ¼ cup of brown sugar (light variety)
- ¼ cup of granulated sugar
- ¼ tsp. salt
- 1 tsp. vanilla
- 1 ½ shredded coconut (sweetened)
- 2 ¼ cups of quick oats
- 1 ¾ cups of rice krispies

Directions

1)   Prepare to dry the strawberries. Preheat the oven to about 200 degrees.

2)   Prepare a large sized baking tray and line it with parchment or wax paper. Distribute the strawberries evenly on the tray with the cut sides facing upward. Bake it for about 2 hours. Remove and flip with the cut sides facing downward this time. Bake it again for another 2 hours. Turn off the oven. Strawberries should look smaller now because it had shrunk already. However, they should still look dark red in color and still feels squishy when you touch it. Bring them back inside the oven and let it sit there until ready to use.

3)   Using an 11x7 inch sized baking tray, line it with aluminum foil. Chop the dried strawberries coarsely.

4)   Using a large sized microwaveable bowl, add coconut oil brown

sugar, corn syrup salt and granulated sugar. Cook inside microwave over high heat for about 90 seconds. Remove and stir it well. Repeat the same process then add vanilla extract.

5)   In a different large sized bowl, add shredded coconuts, dried strawberries rice krispies and oats. Toss them well to combine it evenly. Add sugar mixture. Combine well. Place them on the tray and press them down firmly, make sure that it's compact and firm. Cover it with a plastic wrap. Refrigerate and cut into square pieces.

Nutritious Homemade Granola Bars

Ingredients

- 1 cup of dates (pitted)

- ¼ cup of honey (you can also use agave or maple syrup)

- ¼ cups of peanut butter natural style (salted and creamy variety)

- 1 cup of almonds (unsalted, roasted and chopped loosely)

- 1 ½ cups of rolled oats (you can also use gluten free)

- Choco chips, nuts, vanilla, banana chips, dried fruits (these are optional add ons to your granola bars)

Directions

1) Using a food processor, place the dates and process them coarsely for about a minute. There should be bits remaining to add texture. Upon processing, this should have a dough like form and consistency.

2) This is an optional step: you can toast oats on an oven set to 350 degrees for 15 minutes or until it would turn a bit brown but not burned. But you can choose to leave the oats raw.

3) Place your oats, dates and almonds on a bow and set aside.

4) Using a small sized saucepan, heat the peanut butter and honey over low to medium heat. Stir it well then pour it over the oat mixture. Mix well and make sure that the dates are thoroughly dispersed.

5) Transfer the mixture in an 8x8 sized pan that is already lined with parchment or wax paper so you can take them out easily.

6) Press down firmly and make sure that it is compact. Cover again with parchment or wax paper and place them inside the refrigerator or freezer for about 15-20 minutes to set.

7) Remove from refrigerator and cut them into 10 bars.

8)   Keep them on a container and if needed, get a few pieces and enjoy!

Sweet, Chewy & Crunchy Homemade Bars

Ingredients

- ¾ cup of almonds (unsalted and raw)
- 1/3 cups walnuts (unsalted and raw)
- ¼ cup of brazil nuts (unsalted and raw)
- 1/3 cup of peanuts (salted and roasted)
- ¼ cup of puff rice cereals (you can also use other puffed cereals)
- ½ tablespoon of flaxseed
- ¼ cup of blueberries (dried)
- 3 tablespoons of honey
- 3 tablespoons of brown rice syrup
- ½ teaspoon of vanilla
- ¼ teaspoon of sea salt

Directions

1)   Preheat your oven to 350 degrees.

2)   Grease your spatula and a large sized bowl with a baking spray or a nonstick spray.

3)   Prepare an 8x8 sized baking pan and line it with parchment or wax paper. Arrange walnuts, Brazil nuts and almonds on single layer in the baking sheet. Bake it for about 10 minutes in the oven until it becomes toasted and gets fragrant.

4)   Chop the peanuts and toasted nuts coarsely then place them on a bowl. Add cereals, dried blueberries and flaxseed. Mix them well.

5)   In a medium sized saucepan, put brown rice syrup and honey. Heat mixture to medium-high setting and put a candy thermometer. Once the heat reaches 260 degrees add salt and vanilla quickly then

pour it over the nuts. Mix well.

6)   Put the mixture on the baking pan and press it firmly. Make sure to compress the mixture as much as possible. Set aside on room temperature for at least 20 minutes.

7)   Once mixture already hardened, remove from baking pan and cut to 10 bars.

8)   Keep on individual wraps so that they won't get sticky. Enjoy!

Nuts and Dried Fruit Granola Bars

Ingredients

- 2 cups of rolled oats
- 1/3 cup of pumpkin seeds (raw)
- 1 cup chopped almonds
- ¼ cups of wheat germ
- ¼ cup of flax seed (ground)
- ¼ cup of coconut (shredded)
- ¼ cup of honey
- ¼ cup of agave nectar
- ¼ cup of brown sugar (dark variety)
- 1 tbs. butter
- 1 tbs. coconut oil
- 2 tablespoons of vanilla extract
- ½ teaspoon of Kosher salt or sea salt
- 1 cup dried fruit (chopped)

Directions

1)   Grease using butter a 9x13 glass baking pan. Set aside.

2)   Preheat your over to 350 degrees

3)   Spread and place the pumpkin seeds, oats, almonds, flax seeds and wheat germ to the half sheet pan. Cook and toast in the oven for about 15 minutes. Stir it occasionally. During the last minutes, add shredded coconut and toast it again lightly.

4)   Combine agave nectar, honey, brown sugar, coconut oil, butter, salt and vanilla extract in a medium sized saucepan. Cook over low to

medium heat until the sugar is completely dissolved.

5)   Once the oats are cooked, remove from oven and reduce the heat of the oven to 300 degrees. Mix this oat mixture with the cooked liquid mixture and add dried fruits. Combine well. Pour over the prepared baking pan and press down firmly. Make sure to spread it evenly and bake for about 25 minutes. Once it is cooked, allow to cool and place inside the refrigerator for about 20-30 minutes.

6)   When the mixture is completely hardened, flip the pan over the chopping board and cut it to bars. This will make about 4-6 bars.

7)   Keep them on a container and if needed, get a few pieces and enjoy!

Sweet Peppermint Bars with Dates

Ingredients

- 1 cup of packed dates (pitted)

- 1 cup of rolled oats

- 2 tablespoons of cocoa powder

- ¼ cup of protein powder (unflavored)

- ¼ teaspoon of fine sea salt for tasting

- 2 tablespoons of almond milk

- ½ teaspoon of peppermint extract

- ½ cup of walnuts

- ¼ cup of almonds

- 1 tablespoon of millet (this is optional)

- 4 tablespoon of mini dark choco chops

- 1-2 tablespoon of coconut (unsweetened and large flakes)

Directions

1)   Prepare a baking pan and line it with just 2 pieces of parchment or wax paper, each of them going the other way. Set aside.

2)   Using a food processor, pulse the dates until it becomes sticky.

3)   Add the rolled oats, protein powder, salt, cocoa powder, almond milk and peppermint extract. Process it well and scrape the sides of the bowl if it's needed.

4)   Add nuts, choco chips and millet (if you will be adding one). Pulse again until it is combined well and becomes sticky. This is important to form mixture into balls.

5)   Crumble the mixture you made in the pan. Sprinkle a good amount of coconut flakes on top and press it slightly using your wet

fingers. Cover it with wax or parchment paper. Roll using a pastry roller to smoothen.

6)   Freeze the said mixture for about 15 minutes or until it is hardened. Once done, slice and cut. This would make at least 12 small bars.

7)   Keep them on a container and if needed, get a few pieces and enjoy!

Blueberry and Banana Protein Bars

Ingredients

- 3 eggs (organic preferred)
- 2 pieces of ripe bananas (mashed)
- 1/3 cup of maple syrup
- ¼ cup of non-dairy milk
- 1 teaspoon of vanilla extract
- 1 cup of protein powder
- ½ cup of oatmeal (you can also use oat brans)
- ½ cup of coconut flour
- ½ cup of flax meal
- 2 cups of blueberries (you can either use frozen or fresh)

Directions

1)   Preheat your oven to 180 degrees. Line and grease a 23 centimeter square cake tray then set aside.

2)   Using a large sized bowl, beat eggs, maple syrup, banana, vanilla extract and milk until it's well blended.

3)   Using another medium bowl, mix the protein powder, oatmeal, coconut flour and flax meal. Add the wet ingredients to the dry ones and combine them well.

4)   Bake for at least 30 minutes or until you can see that the top is already browned a little. If you also check and place a toothpick on the middle, it should come out without any marks. This means that the mixture is already cooked.

5)   Cool this completely. Once cooled, you can already cut into 12 bars.

6) Place it on a container and grab whenever needed. Enjoy!

Chewy & Nutty Energy Bars

Ingredients

- 1 cup of oatmeal

- ½ cup of almonds

- ½ cup of pistachios

- 1/3 cup of cranberries

- 2 tablespoons of flaxseeds (ground)

- 2 tbs. chia seeds

- ½ cup of clover honey

Directions

1)   Prepare an 8x8 sized baking pan and line it with wax or parchment paper. You can also grease the baking pan if you prefer.

2)   Using a medium sized bowl, mix in the oatmeal, almonds, pistachios, cranberries, flaxseeds and chia seeds.

3)   Place the honey in a small sized sauce pan and let it boil. Reduce to low heat and simmer it for about 5 minutes. Make sure to stir it frequently so that it will not burn.

4)   Get 1/3 cup of the boiled honey and carefully pour it in the nuts-seed mixture. Quickly mix to thoroughly combine. Continue adding honey until you have reached your desired taste preference.

5)   Press down firmly this mixture on the prepared pan. Let it cool completely. Or place it inside the refrigerator for about 10-15 minutes.

6)   Once mixture is already set, cut them into bars and then keep them in a container or wrap them individually for your convenience. This makes 12 bars. Enjoy!

Triple Choco-Oatmeal Cookie Bars

Ingredients

- 3 ½ cups of rolled oats

- 4 scoops of protein powder (chocolate flavor)

- ¾ cups of sweetener

- 3 ounces of Greek yogurt (fat free and plain variety)

- 2 large sized eggs

- ½ of avocado

- 1 teaspoon of vanilla extract

- 1 cup of unsweetened applesauce

- 2 tablespoons of chocolate syrup (sugar free)

- 10 tablespoons of cocoa powder

- ¼ tsp. salt

- 2 tsp. baking powder

Directions

1)   Using a blender or food processor, place 2 cups of rolled oats inside and process until turning them into flour.

2)   Once done, add the protein powder, sweetener, Greek yogurt, eggs, avocado, vanilla extract, applesauce and chocolate syrup with the oat flour. Mix and combine well using the same food processor. Add the remaining 1 ½ cups of rolled oats but this time don't process them.

3)   Prepare your baking sheet and grease it with nonstick spray. Scoop your mixture and form them to cookie balls or bars.

4)   Bake for about 10-15 minutes on a 350 degree heat. Once done remove from oven and cool. This would make around 4-8 bars

depending on the size you want.

5)   Keep on an airtight container or wrap them on individual packs so you can take them everywhere.

Peanut Butter and Oatmeal Honey Bars

Ingredients

- 3 cups of rolled oats (you can also use gluten free oats)
- 1 cup of rice krispies
- ¼ cup of peanuts (roasted and chopped)
- ½ teaspoon of sal
- ½ tsp. baking soda
- 1/3 cup of honey
- ½ cup of peanut butter plus additional 2 tablespoons (divided)
- 2 tablespoons of pure coconut oil
- 1 tsp. vanilla extract
- ½ tablespoon of brown sugar

Directions

1)   Preheat your oven to about 350 degrees. Prepare a 9x13 baking glass dish that is lined with wax or parchment paper.

2)   Combine peanuts, rice krispies, oats, baking soda and salt in a medium mixing bowl. Using a microwaveable bowl, place in the ½ cup of peanut butter, honey and coconut oil. Place inside the microwave and heat for about 30 seconds to a minute. Stir and add brown sugar and vanilla.

3)   Combine the wet and dry ingredients. Transfer the mixture on the dish and firmly press down. Make sure that it's compact and evenly distributed over the baking dish.

4)   Microwave your remaining 2 tablespoons peanut butter for about 30 seconds. Drizzle them on top of the bar mixture.

5)   Bake in the oven for about 20-25 minutes. Bars should have a golden brown on its top. Remove from the oven and let cool for about 10-20 minutes. Once cooled, remove from baking dish and cut to serving pieces while it's still firm but soft. This would make around 12 bars

6)   Place the bars to cool on a rack. When it's completely cooled, keep on an airtight container or wrap them individually for your convenience. Enjoy!

Dark Chocolate with Pretzel Bars

Ingredients

- 2 cups of rolled oats

- ¼ cup of pecans (chopped roughly)

- ¼ cup of butter

- ¼ cups brown sugar

- ¼ cup of maple syrup

- ¼ cup of peanut butter (you can use either natural or sweetened variety)

- 2 tsp. vanilla

- ¾ cups of rice cereal (puffed variety)

- ¾ cups of pretzels (chopped roughly

- ¼ cup of dark choco chips

Directions

1) Preheat your oven for 375 degrees.

2) Spread your pecans and oats on your baking tray and roast it for about 10-15 minutes until it becomes golden brown.

3) Whisk sugar, peanut butter, maple syrup and butter on a saucepan in medium-high heat. Whisk them well. Once it becomes warm and combined thoroughly, remove them from the heat and add salt and vanilla.

4) Using a large-sized mixing bowl, mix together pecans, pretzels, oats, puffed rice cereals and chocolate chips. Add the mixture of warm peanut butter and combine them well.

5) Transfer the combined mixture on a 9x9 sized baking pan. Make sure to line it first with aluminum foil. Press it down firmly. Once done, cover it with a greased foil on top and press down again firmly.

6)   Freeze for about 20-30 minutes. Cut to serving portions and enjoy! This would make 8-10 bars.

7)   Keep in a container or wrap them individually for convenience and longer shelf life.

Protein Rich Banana Bread Bars

Ingredients

- 2/3 cup of rolled oats (choose the gluten free variety)
- ½ cup of buckwheat groats (raw & ground it to flour consistency)
- ½ cup of walnuts (chopped)
- ¼ cup of dried coconut (shredded and unsweetened)
- 3 tablespoons of chia seeds
- 3 tablespoons of dark choco chips (mini's)
- ¼ teaspoon of cinnamon
- ¼ teaspoon of sea salt
- ¾ cup of ripe bananas (mashed)
- ½ cup of peanut butter (creamy and natural)
- ¼ cup of syrup (you can choose between brown rice or coconut nectar)
- 1 tsp. vanilla

Directions:

1) Preheat your oven to 350 degrees.

2) Prepare an 8x8 inch sized square pan and line it using a parchment or wax paper.

3) Place the raw groats in a blender and blend on high speed. Remember the consistency has to be like flour. Once it's done, mix oats, walnuts, shredded coconut, chia seeds, choco chips, cinnamon and sea salt. Combine well.

4) Mash the bananas until smooth. Add peanut butter, syrup and vanilla extract. Mix well. When all of the ingredients are combined well, add the oat mixture. Mix them well again.

5)   Once the banana mixture and oat mixture are combined, they will form a dough. This should be very sticky. Pour the dough and place it on the prepared pan. Spread evenly and firmly press it down. Make sure that it's compact as much as possible.

6)   Bake in the oven for about 20-26 minutes or until edges have become golden brown. Bread should also feel firm when you touch it. Remove from the oven and let it cool.

7)   When it's already cool, remove from pan and cut into bars. This would make 10 bars. Keep in a container or wrap them individually for your convenience. Enjoy!

No Bake Vegan & Gluten Free Protein Bars

Ingredients

- 1 ½ cups of oat flour (gluten free)

- 6 dried apricots

- ¼ cup of cocoa powder

- ¼ cup of brown rice syrup

- ½ cup of rolled oats (gluten free)

- ½ cup of protein powder (you can choose vegan chocolate for this)

- ¼ teaspoon of sea salt

- 1 ½ teaspoons of chia seeds

- 1 ½ tablespoons of hemp seeds

- ½ cup of peanut butter

- 1 flax egg

- 1 tablespoon of ground flax

- ¼ cup of agave nectar (you can also use raw honey)

- ½ cup of coconut milk

- 1/3 cup of vegan choco chips

- 1 tablespoon of hemp seeds

Directions

1)   Combine oat flour, apricots, cocoa powder and brown rice syrup in a processor. Pulse and combine until ingredients forms into a thick and crumbly dough. Put it on a bowl and set aside.

2)   On a large sized bowl, combine your dry ingredients to use in the next layer. Use your fork to mix it well.

3)   Mix water and flax in a small sized bowl. Stir it and set aside until mixture starts to become a gel.

4)   Add agave, coconut milk, flax egg and peanut butter on your dried ingredients. Roughly mix using your fork and add it on the food processor. Blend until it becomes smooth. Add some more coconut milk if mixture is very dry. This should look sticky and thick when done.

5)   Prepare an 8x8 sized baking pan and line it with wax or parchment paper. Put the crust mixture and press it down evenly. Make sure that it's compact as much as possible. Place the next layer on top of the crust and spread evenly. Place it on the refrigerator for about an hour.

6)   To prepare for the drizzle, melt 1/3 cup of the choco chips in your double broiler or microwave.

7)   Once the mixture is already hard and set, cut into serving bars. Drizzle choco syrup on top and sprinkle some hemp seeds. This will make around 10-12 bars.

8)   Keep them on a container or wrap them individually for your convenience. Enjoy!

No Bake Granolas with M&M, Pretzels and Peanut Butter

Ingredients

- 2 cups of oats

- 1 cup of rice Krispies

- ½ cup of pretzels (chopped)

- ¼ cup of mimi M&M's (add more to sprinkle)

- ¼ cup of butter

- ¼ cup of honey

- ¼ cup of peanut butter

- ¼ cup of brown sugar (dark variant)

- 1 teaspoon of vanilla extract

Directions

1)   Prepare an 8x8 sized baking pan and line it with wax or parchment paper.

2)   On a large sized bowl, mix rice krispies, oats, m&ms and pretzels. Set aside.

3)   Using a medium saucepan, melt honey, peanut butter, sugar and butter. Bring to boil and let it simmer for 2-3 minutes on medium-high heat. Stir it continuously. Remove from the oven before adding vanilla extract.

4)   Pour the sauce mixture on the dried ingredients and mix well. Make sure that everything is combined well and evenly coated.

5)   When all ingredients are thoroughly combined, pour on baking pan and press down firmly. Make sure to press it down firmly to make it more compact. Sprinkle a few more additional m&ms press it down again but a bit more lightly this time.

6) Refrigerate for about 30 minutes. When the mixture is already set, cut into serving pieces. This would make 10 bars.

7) Keep on a container or wrap them individually so you can go ahead and bring them along. Enjoy!

No Bake White Choco Protein Bars

Ingredients

- 1 ½ cup of oats

- ½ cup of peanut butter (natural variant)

- 1/3 cup maple syrup (plus additional 1 tablespoon)

- 1 tablespoon of hemp seed

- 1 tablespoon of chia seeds

- ¼ cup protein powder (you can choose what flavor you want or you can use vegan)

- ¼ cups of white choco chips (you can also use vegan white chocolate)

- 2 tablespoons of white choco chips to be used for drizzling

Directions

1)   In a medium sized bowl, mix oats, peanut butter, hemp seeds, chia seeds, maple syrup and protein powder. Mix them all well.

2)   Add the ¼ cup of white chocolate and combine thoroughly.

3)   Prepare an 8x8 sized baking pan and line it with wax or parchment paper.

4)   Spread the mixture evenly and press it down firmly.

5)   Melt the 2 tablespoons of white choco inside the microwave or a saucepan. Drizzle on top of your mixture.

6)   Place them inside the freezer for 30 min. or just until it's set. Once done, remove from freezer and cut them in 12 bars.

7)   Keep in a container that's air tight or wrap them individually for your convenience. Enjoy!

Buckwheat and Blueberry Granola Bars

Ingredients

- 2 cups of rolled oats
- 1 cup of buckwheat groats (raw)
- 1 cup of dried blueberries
- ½ cup of almonds (slivered)
- ½ cup of puffed millet (you can also use brown rice)
- ¼ cup of chia seeds
- ¼ cup of hemp seeds
- 1 tsp. cinnamon
- ¼ tsp. cardamom
- ½ cup of raw almond butter (use the unsalted and creamy variant)
- ½ cup of maple syrup (pure)
- 1/3 cup of coconut oil
- 2 teaspoons of vanilla extract
- ¼ teaspoon of sea salt (fine grain)

Directions

1) Using a large sized bowl, mix together buckwheat groats, blueberries, oats, puffed millet, almonds, chia seeds, cinnamon and hemp seeds.

2) Melt maple syrup, almond butter, vanilla extract, salt and coconut oil on a small saucepan for about 3-4 minutes over a low to medium heat until blended together.

3) Prepare a baking tray and line it with wax or parchment paper. Have the edges of the paper stick out on the edges for easier removal

of the mixture.

4)   Pour granola mixture into the tray and press it down firmly. Spread it evenly and make it compact as much as possible.

5)   When the mixture is already pressed down completely and molded together, put the tray inside the freezer and leave for about 30 minutes in order to set.

6)   Once done, remove out of the tray and prepare your cutting board. Slice them into 20 delicious bars.

7)   Keep in an airtight container or wrap them individually for your convenience. Enjoy!

Hemp Protein Rich Granola Bars

Ingredients

- 1 ½ cups of rolled oats
- ¾ cup of walnuts (chopped; you can also use other kinds of nut)
- 1 cup of chopped dates; you can also use other dried fruits
- 1 cup of flaked coconuts
- ½ cup powder of hemp protein
- ¼ cup of sesame seeds
- 2 tablespoons of poppy seeds
- 2 tsp. cinnamon
- ½ tsp. salt
- 3 pieces of ripe bananas
- ¼ cup of sunflower oil
- 2 teaspoons of vanilla extract
- 3 tablespoons of maple syrup
- 2 tablespoons of chia seeds
- 6 tablespoons of water

Directions

1) Preheat your oven to 350 degrees.

2) Using a small sized bowl, mix water and chia seeds then set aside.

3) Meanwhile, using a large sized bowl combine dry ingredients.

4) Using a blender or food processor, blend the bananas, vanilla,

maple syrup and oil. Add reserved chia gel and mix. Combine all the wet ingredients with the dry ingredients. Mix them thoroughly.

5)   Pour the mixture on your pan, spread and press down firmly. Bake for about 20-25 minutes or until you can see that the edges turned golden brown. Remove from the oven and cool. You can also freeze for about an hour until it is completely set. Slice into serving portions. This would make around6-8 bars.

6)   Keep on an airtight container or wrap individually for your convenience. Enjoy!

Protein Pumpkin Bread Bars

Ingredients

- 2 eggs
- ½ cup of honey
- 1 cup of pumpkin
- 2 tsp. vanilla
- 1 ½ cup of unflavored protein powder
- ¼ cup all-purpose flour
- ½ tsp. baking soda
- ¼ tsp. baking powder
- 1 tsp. pumpkin spice
- ¼ tsp. cloves (ground)
- ½ teaspoon of cinnamon
- ¼ teaspoon of salt

Directions

1)   Combine first all the wet ingredients and then followed by the dry ingredients.

2)   Combine well and pour them on an 8x8 greased baking pan.

3)   Bake for about 25-30 minutes or until you can see the edges already crisp and brown. Let cool.

4)   Once the bread is already cool, cut them into 10 or 12 square slices.

5)   Wrap them individually and enjoy!

Conclusion

Thank you for reading this book until the end. I hope that you've had a wonderful time preparing and creating these delicious and nutritious bars in the comfort of your home. People on the go need to have proper nutrition so what better way than easy DIY protein bars. It's also best that you know what you are eating. You have to take care of your body despite the overabundance of processed foods.

These protein bars, granola bars or energy bars, as what they are commonly called, are good replacements especially if you are always on the go. Instead of eating processed foods or chips, you might as well eat these treats and satisfy your hunger.

A good tip is to set one day during the weekend to bake all of the granola protein bars you need for the week. During the weekdays, grab some bars when you are hungry. Pack yourself a number of bars to help you get through the day without being hungry.

However, these bars are not there to replace your full meal. While they are rich in protein and other good nutrients, take note that you still need to eat a proper diet. Protein bars are meant for quick bursts of energy and for easy and effective replenishment pre and post workout..

Having said that, again it's always a pleasure sharing with you my delicious recipes. I hope that you have learned a lot from this book.

Have a happy, healthy life!

To hear about Jessica's new books first (and to be notified when there are free promotions), sign up to her New Release Mailing List.

Finally, if you enjoyed this book, please take the time to share your thoughts and post a review on Amazon. It'd be greatly appreciated!

Thank you and good luck!

Preview Of 'Vegetarian Diet: 41 Phenomenal Vegetarian Recipes for Clean Eating, Losing Weight and Staying Healthy' by Jessica David

Chapter One: Five Basic Meal Types

We all know the old way of thinking about food. Mealtime.

In today's hectic world, there is a completely different way to think about caloric intake. When we consider what the purposes are for eating, it can impact everything from the kinds of food we eat to the style of meal we find acceptable. Below we introduce the real core reasons people eat, and how each one can be dealt with in a whole new way.

In this chapter, you will learn:

- A new way to think about eating

- Food fascination and how to overcome it.

Eating as a Necessity

Eating is the body's way of re-charging, of getting prepared for specific actions, and for sustenance, keeping the body functioning. The clearest point of this kind of eating tends to be at the end of a sleeping period, generally the longest period of non-sustaining ingestion. Thinking in these terms, therefore, one must consider what foods are the best for driving up metabolism, getting the body into a mode for functioning.

Fast-Breakers

Some foods that are particularly great for this are quick carbohydrates, complex grains for fiber, and slow proteins, to give that metabolism something to work on. Historically, breakfast foods meet these kinds of conditions rather well. We will go over some quick alternatives that will get you going, and grant you the energy you need to get on with the day.

Eating as a Function

As with breakfast time, there are points in the day where you simply need a re-charge, a jump-start, or a quick pick-me-up. Generally, snack foods are the sole foodstuff that is looked for in these circumstances, but instead we recommend a reconsideration of alternatives. Vegetables and slow-metabolizing fruits and simpler grains meet these needs better, and provide a greater range of flavors and options.

Grab n Go

Eating while moving has been a part of human activity from the ancient hunter-and-gatherer days. Take advantage of the options and alternatives to make your day a continuously-active metabolism, so your desires for food become sheer necessity, not impulsive snacking. This kind of lifestyle change will lead to a greater appreciation of your time, as well as weight loss and less stress over the foods you eat.

Eating as Socialization

It isn't always about intake. We as human beings enjoy the company for others, and the draw to be together when eating is an ancient appeal. It may even be that this is how we as a species discovered what was edible, and what was not.

Taste Triggers

Our need to be together gives us a great opportunity to expand our dietary repertoire. Using such as a basis for communal meals can give us more than just sustenance, and our communication can become the center point, rather than the intake of food itself... meaning we grow together more closely, and the things we talk about can have more direct impact on our lives, as it is more clearly focused on our collective survival.

Eating for Survival

Particularly when we are in our developing years, the sheer need to eat can take precedence, become a critical point in existence. With that in mind, we can look differently at those points, those times, and perhaps use them as they should be, for those that need them. Children who are growing constantly, as well as those who are ill should consider not only what they eat that can assist in the process, but also the very volume itself.

Vital Volume
Fiber, Protein, Vitamins, and more make up our regular diet. If we consider our internal condition, sometimes certain foods need to be eaten in larger or more precise volumes to overcome affliction, or to enhance growth and development. Keeping track of these conditions can even improve our health in an overall manner as well.

Eating as Experience
Perhaps the most encouraging and enjoyable kind of eating is when it is solely for the enjoyment of it. When we consider this as the sole purpose, we can see that it need not be at high volume or of particularly strong savor. Eating to taste the food is itself an appealing and necessary part of the diet process.

Food Fascination
Some people have an affinity for a particular fruit. Others, for chocolate or root beer. By searching out food alternatives that can parallel foods that you had eaten in an earlier diet pattern can assist you in overcoming certain diet-killing cravings. So use this skill, this passion, this desire to expand and more broadly define what it is that appeals to you, and discover ways that you can sate this need in other forms, to give yourself a better chance to remain in the diet restrictions, without feeling deprived of the foods you desire.

In a traditional recipe book, you are given strict creation instructions for making particular dishes. This book, instead, offers broader alternatives within the whole of foods available that will keep you in a vegetarian diet, but that instead looks at foods as resources to draw against in an attempt to make a sustainable diet change not only possible, but a natural transition.

Click here to check out the rest of Vegetarian Diet: 41 Phenomenal Vegetarian Recipes for Clean Eating, Losing Weight and Staying Healthy on Amazon.

Or go to: http://amzn.to/1JI8GU1

More Books On Food, Health and Wellness

Click here to check out the rest of <u>Jessica's books on Amazon</u>.

Below you'll find some of my other popular books that are popular on Amazon and Kindle as well. Simply click on the links below to check them out. Alternatively, you can visit my author page on Amazon to see other work done by me.

<u>Nutribullet Superfood: 31 Heavenly Nutribullet Soup Recipes You</u>

Can't Blend Without

Nutribullet Superfood: The Secret Of A 7 Day Smoothies Detox Using Natural Healing Foods

Nutribullet Superfood: 40 Protein Packed Power Smoothie Recipes To Help You Lose Weight And Build Lean Muscle (Includes: Bonus Protein Add-Ins Guide)

Nutribullet Superfood: 37 Luscious Fruit Smoothie Recipes For A Pleasurable And Healthy Summer

Nutribullet Superfood: 4-in-1 Smoothie Recipe Book Boxed Set

Dash Diet: 100 Dash Diet Snacks And Recipes: Ready In 20 Minutes Or Less (Perfect For Beginners)

Apple Cider Vinegar For Weight Loss: The Secret Of A Successful Natural Remedy For Faster Weight Loss

Coconut Oil For Weight Loss: The Secret Of An Ancient Essential Oil For Faster Weight Loss

Apple Cider Vinegar and Coconut Oil for Weight Loss: 2-in-1 Secret Essential Oil And Successful Natural Remedy For Faster Weight Loss Boxed Set

Baby Powder: 17 Impressive Uses for Baby Powder You've Never Considered

Sprinting For Weight Loss: How To Achieve An Accelerated Metabolism And Lose Weight Fast In Just 10 Minutes A Day

Mediterranean Diet Recipes: 37 Mouth Watering Mediterranean Diet Recipes For Weight Loss And Vigorous Heart Health

Vegetarian Diet: 41 Phenomenal Vegetarian Recipes for Clean Eating, Losing Weight and Staying Healthy

If the links do not work, for whatever reason, you can simply search for these titles on the Amazon website to find them.

Made in the USA
Middletown, DE
13 August 2018